WHY DO WE SAY THAT?

101 Idioms, Phrases, Sayings & Facts! The Origins & History Of Your Favorite Colloquial Terms, Expressions, Phrases & Proverbs

---

SCOTT MATTHEWS

Copyright © 2023 Scott Matthews

All rights reserved. No part of this publication may be reproduced, distributed or transmitted in any form or by any means, including photocopying, recording, or other electronic or mechanical methods, without the prior written permission of the publisher, except in the case of brief quotations embodied in critical reviews and certain other non-commercial uses permitted by copyright law.

Trademarked names appear throughout this book. Rather than use a trademark symbol with every occurrence of a trademarked name, names are used in an editorial fashion, with no intention of infringement of the respective owner's trademark. The information in this book is distributed on an "as is" basis, without warranty. Although every precaution has been taken in the preparation of this work, neither the author nor the publisher shall have any liability to any person or entity with respect to any loss or damage caused or alleged to be caused directly or indirectly by the information contained in this book.

The more that you read, the more things you will know. The more you learn, the more places you'll go. - Dr. Seuss

Contents

Introduction	vii
1. Kill two birds with one stone	1
2. Draw a blank	2
3. Keeping up with the Joneses	3
4. Palm off	4
5. Frog in one's throat	5
6. Get hitched	6
7. Monkey business	7
8. Lo and behold	8
9. No pain, no gain	9
10. All bark and no bite	10
11. Know the ropes	12
12. Runs the gamut/Run the gauntlet	13
13. Zero-sum game	15
14. Eat like a horse	16
15. Snake-oil salesman	17
16. Blow off steam	18
17. Take the mickey out of someone	19
18. Cheap as chips	20
19. Storm in a teacup	21
20. Put something on ice	22
21. The leopard never changes its spots	24
22. Blow smoke	25
23. Third time's the charm	26
24. Hook line and sinker	27
25. To pitch in	28
26. It's not rocket science	29
27. In the loop and out of the loop	30
28. Waste not, want not	31
29. Twist someone's arm	32
30. Witch hunt	33
31. Not all it's cracked up to be	35
32. A class act	36
33. Snug as a bug in a rug	37

34. A little bird told me	38
35. A penny saved is a penny earned	39
36. Actions speak louder than words	40
37. Blue once a month	41
38. To bell the cat	42
39. Dig one's heels in	43
40. The best thing since sliced bread	44
41. Under the table	46
42. Not your cup of tea	47
43. To get on like a house on fire	48
44. Close, but no cigar	49
45. No horse in the race	50
46. Under the weather	51
47. Good things come to those who wait	52
48. Turn a deaf ear	53
49. Fish story	54
50. Flesh and blood	55
51. To be on the same wavelength	57
52. Every nook and cranny	58
53. Eat like a bird	59
54. Straw that broke the camel's back	60
55. Bounce something off someone	61
56. We'll cross that bridge when we get to it	62
57. Don't rain on my parade	63
58. Take a rain check	64
59. Shoot oneself in the foot	65
60. Hold your horses	66
61. Raise one's hackles	68
62. Don't put all your eggs in one basket	69
63. Between a rock and a hard place	70
64. Sit on the fence	71
65. To cut someone some slack	72
66. Spice things up	73
67. To get a second wind	74
68. Elbow grease	75
69. Smoke and mirrors	76
70. Give them a run for their money	77
71. See a man about a dog	79
72. Get off your high horse	80
73. Scratch someone's back	81
74. Put something on the map	82

75. Scrape the barrel	83
76. A watched pot never boils	84
77. Between the devil and the deep blue sea	85
78. Bite the hand that feeds you	86
79. By the book	87
80. Keep your chin up	88
81. Make hay while the sun shines	90
82. Not a snowball's chance in hell	91
83. Out of the frying pan and into the fire	92
84. Read someone like a book	93
85. The devil you know is better than the devil you don't	94
86. The shoe is on the other foot	95
87. Turn over a new leaf	96
88. Walking on air	97
89. Wear your heart on your sleeve	98
90. When it rains, it pours	99
91. Zero in on something	101
92. Burning the candle at both ends	102
93. Count your blessings	103
94. Every dog has its day	104
95. Fish or cut bait	105
96. Hit the ground running	106
97. Keep something at bay	107
98. Like shooting fish in a barrel	108
99. Make a long story short	109
100. Off the beaten path	110
101. One man's trash is another man's treasure	112

Introduction

Are you ready to explore the intriguing world of idioms? You might be surprised to learn that we use them daily, sometimes without even realizing it! But have you ever wondered about the origins of these fascinating phrases?

Also called idiomatic expressions, idioms have slowly been introduced into the English language as it has developed over time. These expressions have a commonly understood meaning which varies from the literal meaning of the words being spoken, read, or written.

As we explore the origins of idioms, we'll be taking a journey back in time to discover what the English-speaking world was like when these phrases were first used. While some idioms have clear origins, others have evolved over time, passed down through oral tradition, and may have unknown origins or multiple theories of where they came from. Despite this, the enduring popularity and widespread use of these idioms continue to pique our interest and inspire further inquiry.

So let's dive right into the wonderful world of idioms and where they come from!

1. Kill two birds with one stone

Sources believe that this phrase originated from the Greek mythology story of Daedalus and Icarus, where Daedalus killed two birds with one stone to get their feathers in order to make wings. The expression first appeared in writing in 1656, in *The Questions Concerning Liberty, Necessity, and Chance by Thomas Hobbes*, where he wrote, "T.H. thinks to kill two birds with one stone, and satisfies two arguments with one answer, whereas in truth he satisfieth neither." Today, the idiom is used more broadly to mean to accomplish two things simultaneously or in a single effort, often in an efficient or cost-effective manner. It is often used to suggest that it is possible to achieve multiple goals or objectives with a single action or effort rather than having to devote separate resources or time to each task.

2. Draw a blank

The expression "draw a blank" is a colloquial way of describing when someone is unable to remember or recall something, or when someone is not able to find the information they are looking for. The origins of this phrase can be traced back to the late 19th century and Tudor, England, where the first national lottery was established by Queen Elizabeth in 1567. The operation of the lottery involved the insertion of slips of paper, each bearing the name of a participant, into one container, while an equivalent quantity of slips, some denoting rewards and others being blank, were placed in another receptacle. A simultaneous drawing of pairs of tickets from both containers would result in a pairing between a participant and a prize. However, it was not uncommon for the drawing to produce a blank slip, leading to the participant "drawing a blank" and winning no reward.

3. Keeping up with the Joneses

The expression "keeping up with the Joneses" refers to the act of trying to maintain the same level of material possessions or social status as one's neighbors or peers. It suggests a desire to fit in or be seen as successful or affluent and can often involve spending beyond one's means or engaging in conspicuous consumption to keep up with others. The expression was first used in the 1913 comic *Keeping Up With the Joneses*, created by Arthur R. Momand. The comic centers around the McGinnis family and their constant endeavor to keep up with their neighbors, the Joneses. The Joneses remained unseen throughout the comic strip, although they were regularly mentioned. As a generic last name, "Jones" has been widely used to identify neighbors and other rivals.

4. Palm off

The term "palm off" refers to a situation in which someone tries to deceive or trick someone else by selling them something of poor quality or by pretending that something is of higher value than it actually is. It is thought to have originated in the 19th century and is likely derived from the idea of "palming off" a fake or inferior object by quickly slipping it into someone's hand without their noticing. Today, the phrase is a common idiom in English and is commonly used to convey a sense of deception or trickery.

5. Frog in one's throat

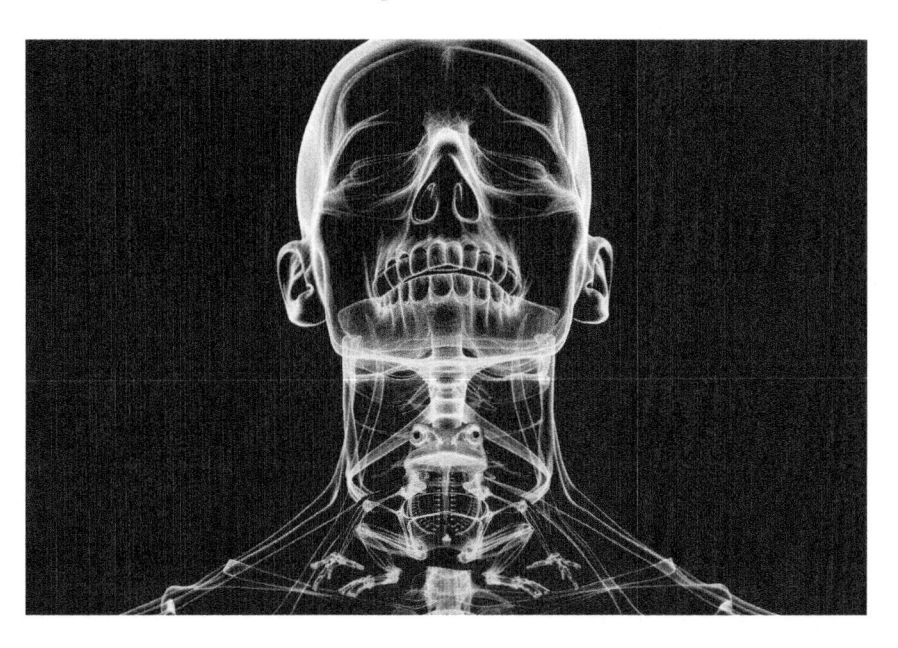

The idiom "frog in one's throat" is used to describe the sensation of having a lump in one's throat or difficulty swallowing or speaking. It originated in the United Kingdom in the 19th century and comes from the idea of a frog being a small, slimy animal that might be difficult to swallow. The phrase suggests that the person in question is experiencing a similar sensation of having something stuck in their throat that is causing difficulty swallowing or speaking. It is often used in a casual or lighthearted manner, implying that the person is experiencing a temporary or minor issue with their throat. However, it can also be used more seriously to describe a more persistent or severe issue with the throat.

6. Get hitched

"Get hitched" is an idiomatic expression that means to get married. The origin of this phrase is unique to America and can be traced back to the mid-1800s. The expression compares getting married to teaming a pair of horses to pull a wagon or farm implement. It implies that the couple is now connected to each other and will work together to pull their life together. The phrase is a metaphor for the act of getting married and it is not meant to be an insult to the people in question; the expression is a testament to their compatibility. The practice of "hitching" a horse or other animal to a wagon or other vehicle in order to pull it was a common practice among farmers who only hitched teams of horses who had matched temperaments or whose temperaments complemented each other's.

7. Monkey business

The expression "monkey business" is rooted in the term "monkeyshine," which originated in 1832 and referred to a dishonorable act. In England, parents warned their children against bad conduct referred to as "monkey tricks." The idiom "monkey business" was first recorded in print in 1883 in W. Peck's Bad Boy, where it was used to warn against any sneaky or underhanded behavior. The phrase implies that the person or people involved are behaving in a way that is mischievous or dishonest and it has been used to describe illegal or unethical activities too.

8. Lo and behold

The idiom "lo and behold" is an expression of surprise and emphasis, and it is often used to introduce something unexpected or remarkable. The phrase is thought to have originated from Middle English, specifically from the phrase "lo, behold!" which was used to express surprise or emphasis. The phrase became popular in the 16th century and has been used widely in literature and everyday speech since then. Both "lo" and "behold" are derived from Old English, with "lo" meaning "look" and "behold" meaning "give regard to" and "belong to." The phrase can be found in the King James Bible in 1611, where it says "And Abraham said; Behold, to mee thou has given no seed: and loe, one borne in my house is mine heire."

9. No pain, no gain

The expression "no pain, no gain" suggests that one must endure discomfort and exert effort in order to achieve a desired outcome, often in reference to building muscle or losing weight. It originated in the 1980s as a catchphrase used by fitness gurus and personal trainers, and is often used to motivate people to continue working hard, even when feeling tired or discouraged. The concept of this phrase can also be found in ancient Greek literature, specifically in the play *Electra* by Sophocles written in the 5th century BC, where it is stated that "Nothing truly succeeds without pain, nothing succeeds without toil, there is no success without hard work." This reinforces the idea that one can't expect to achieve something without putting in the effort.

10. All bark and no bite

The idiom "all bark and no bite" vividly captures the idea of someone who talks tough or boasts confidently, but ultimately fails to follow through with meaningful action. It likens the situation to a dog that barks aggressively but doesn't actually attack. This expression dates back to the 19th century and is believed to have origins in the behavior of animals. Although no specific written record of its earliest use exists, the idiom's metaphorical essence has remained remarkably consistent over time. In contemporary usage, "all bark and no bite" is playfully employed to humorously criticize individuals or situations where grandiose claims or threats lack genuine substance or force. It serves as a gentle reminder that actions speak louder than words, adding a touch of insight and whimsy to conversations about bravado and authenticity.

Did You Know?

- The word "algorithm" comes from the name of the mathematician Al-Khwarizmi, who was a 9th-century Persian scholar. Al-Khwarizmi wrote a book called *Kitab al-Jabr wa-l-Muqabilah*, which means "The Book of Restoration and Balance," which contained a set of rules for solving mathematical problems.
- The word "tycoon" comes from the Japanese "taikun," which means "great lord." It was originally used to refer to the shogun, the military ruler of Japan, but it later came to be used as a term for a wealthy and powerful business person.
- The word "cocktail" comes from the French "coquetier," which means "egg cup." The term originally described a drink that was served in an egg-shaped glass.
- The word "chaos" comes from the Greek "khaos," which means "vast chasm or void." In Greek mythology, Chaos was the personification of the void or the emptiness that existed before the creation of the universe.

11. Know the ropes

To "know the ropes" means to be familiar with the ins and outs of a particular system, procedure, or activity. It suggests that the person has a high level of expertise or experience in a particular area and can navigate it with confidence and skill. This expression came about in the mid-16th to mid-19th centuries when sailing was the most common way of long-distance travel, and knowing how to sail was a highly valued skill. Before steamships were invented, many of a ship's operations were conducted via ropes and pulleys. To "know the ropes" meant that a person knew precisely which ropes had to be used for a specific function.

12. Runs the gamut/Run the gauntlet

The word "gamut" comes from the Latin language and means "the whole range" or "all the notes." It was first used in medieval music theory to describe the range of notes in a diatonic scale, from the lowest to the highest. As music theory evolved, the gamut was divided into smaller parts called hexachords, which were a series of six notes. By the 18th century, the term "gamut" came to be used more metaphorically, to describe a complete range of anything. In other words, if something "runs the gamut" it means it covers all aspects or all the variations of something. The idiom "to run the gauntlet" means to undergo a severe test or punishment, often involving physical abuse. The phrase is thought to have originated in the 17th century and it comes from a military punishment used in the past. In this punishment, a person was made to run between two lines of soldiers who would beat or strike the person as they ran through. This practice is known as "running the gauntlet" and the expression is used to describe any situation in which someone is subjected to severe punishment or harassment.

13. Zero-sum game

The phrase "zero-sum game" is an economic and game theory term used to describe a situation in which one person's gain is directly proportional to another person's loss. It is a situation where the total amount of resources is fixed and any gain by one person results in an equal loss by another person. The expression was first coined by John von Neumann and Oskar Morgenstern in their 1944 book *Theory of Games and Economic Behavior*. The concept of zero-sum game is often used to describe competitive situations such as business, sports, and politics.

14. Eat like a horse

The idiom "eat like a horse" refers to someone who eats a large quantity of food or eats very frequently. It originated in the 19th century and is derived from the observation that horses are known for their ability to eat huge amounts of food. Horses have a unique digestive system that allows them to eat large amounts of food at one time, and to extract the maximum amount of nutrition from it. They have a large stomach that can hold up to fifteen gallons (fifty-seven liters) of food, and they are able to graze for most of the day. In literature and popular culture, this phrase is often used in a humorous or exaggerating way, to convey that someone eats a lot of food, but not always in a negative way. It can also be used to describe someone who is eating in an indiscriminate way, without manners or delicacy.

15. Snake-oil salesman

The term "snake-oil salesman" describes someone who sells fraudulent or ineffective goods or services, with the implication that the salesperson is deceitful and untrustworthy. The expression is derived from the sale of "snake oil," a supposed cure-all that was often hawked by traveling salesmen in the 19th century. The origins of the phrase can be traced back to the early 19th century when Chinese immigrants in America working on the transcontinental railroad brought with them a traditional Chinese remedy for joint pain made from the oil of the Chinese water snake. Salesmen, who were not Chinese, began to sell their own versions of the remedy and often used the oil from other animals such as rattlesnakes, claiming it had the same medicinal properties. These salesmen were known to be dishonest, exaggerating the effectiveness of their products and often using dangerous or ineffective ingredients. As a result, the idiom "snake oil salesman" became synonymous with a con artist who sells fake or ineffective goods.

16. Blow off steam

To "blow off steam" means to release pent-up emotions or energy, often through physical or verbal expression. It is commonly used to describe the act of venting one's feelings or frustrations in order to reduce stress. There are two theories about the origins of this idiom. The first is that it is a reference to the way in which steam is released from a pressure valve in order to prevent an explosion or other catastrophic events. When a pressure valve is released, steam is allowed to escape in a controlled manner, preventing the build-up of pressure that could lead to an explosion. In a similar way, the idiom "blow off steam" may describe the act of releasing pent-up emotions or energy in a controlled manner in order to prevent a build-up of stress or tension. The second theory is that it may be a reference to the way in which steam locomotives release steam through their exhaust pipes in order to move forward. In this context, the idiom may have been used to describe the act of releasing energy or emotions in order to move forward or to relieve tension.

17. Take the mickey out of someone

To "take the mickey out of someone" means to tease or make fun of someone in a playful and good-natured way. It originated in the early 20th century in England, specifically in the Cockney dialect spoken in the East End of London. The word "mickey" is a slang term that was used to refer to a fool or an easy target for teasing. The phrase "taking the mickey" is believed to have come from the expression "taking the Mickey Bliss," which was a reference to a famous music hall song and stage act of the time. The act featured a man dressed as a woman named Mickey Bliss, who was often the butt of jokes and pranks.

18. Cheap as chips

The idiom "as cheap as chips" is a British phrase describing something that is inexpensive. The expression originated from the low cost of fish and chips, a traditional British meal that was popular among working-class people. Fish and chips were a cheap and readily available food item that could be purchased from street vendors or fish and chip shops. The phrase is typically used to indicate that something is very affordable, or that it offers good value for money.

19. Storm in a teacup

A "storm in a teacup" describes a situation that is being blown out of proportion or made to seem more significant or serious than it really is. It originated in the United Kingdom in the 17th century and comes from the idea of a teacup being a small and delicate container that is not capable of holding a large or intense storm. Nowadays, the expression is often used in a casual or lighthearted manner, implying that the situation is not particularly important or worth getting worked up over. Despite its lighthearted tone, the idiom can also be used to express frustration or annoyance with someone who is overreacting or making a big deal out of a minor issue.

20. Put something on ice

The expression "put something on ice" means to delay or postpone, usually temporarily, and can be used in a variety of contexts, such as business, politics, or personal matters. There are two different theories about the origins of this idiom. The first theory is that it comes from the idea of storing food in a cold place, such as a refrigerator or an icebox, in order to preserve it, suggesting that the idiom originally referred to the act of delaying the use or consumption of something by storing it in a cold place. The second theory is that the it is related to the expression "put something on hold," which means to delay or postpone something, suggesting that the idiom originally referred to the act of holding something in a state of inactivity.

Did You Know?

- The word "apocalypse" comes from the Greek "apokalypsis," which means "revelation." It is used to describe a catastrophic event or the end of the world.
- The word "petroleum" comes from the Latin "petra," which means "rock," and "oleum," which means "oil." It refers to a type of oil that is found in rock formations and is used as a fuel and a raw material for a variety of products.
- The word "kiwi" comes from the Maori word "kiwi," which is the name of a flightless bird native to New Zealand. The fruit was given this name because it is native to New Zealand and has a brown, fuzzy skin similar to the skin of the kiwi bird.
- The word "sherbet" comes from the Turkish "şerbet," which means "drink." It refers to a type of sweet, fruity drink that is made from fruit juice, water, and sugar.

21. The leopard never changes its spots

"The leopard never changes its spots" is a proverb that means that people do not change their basic nature or inherent character. The origins of this idiom can be traced back to ancient cultures, where the leopard was recognized as a powerful and majestic animal that was known for its distinctive spots. The saying reflects the belief that people cannot change the fundamental aspects of their personality, just as a leopard cannot change its spots. The phrase was first seen in the Old Testament and was used in Jeremiah 13:23, where the Hebrew prophet Jeremiah said: "Can the Ethiopian change his skin, or the leopard its spots?"

22. Blow smoke

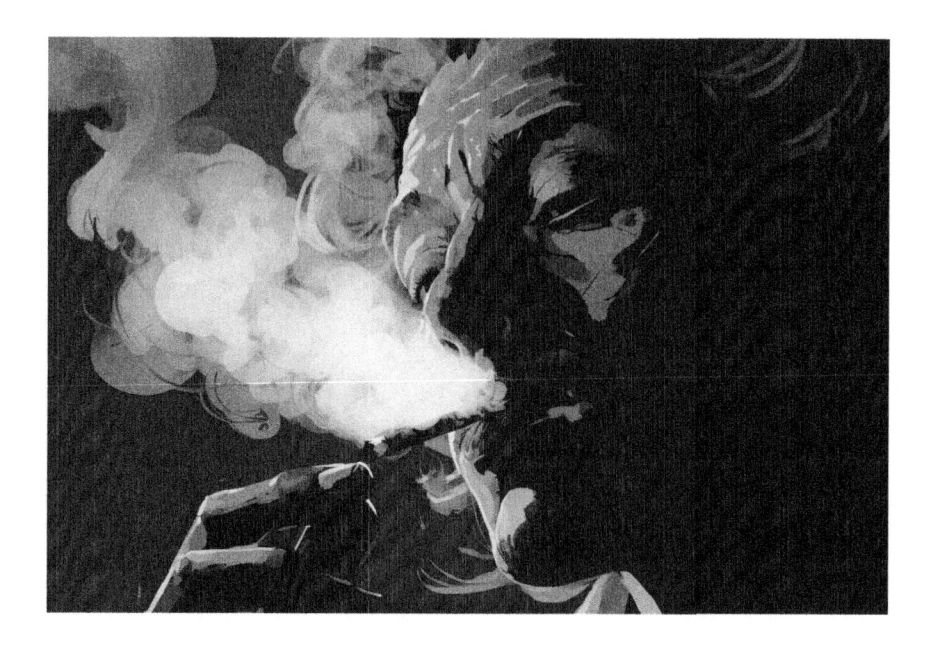

"Blow smoke" is an idiom that means to make false or empty statements or promises, or to deceive or mislead someone. It originated from the act of smoking, as the phrase is often used to describe situations where someone is exhaling smoke from their mouth or nose. In modern usage, the expression describes situations where someone is trying to deceive or mislead others by making false or exaggerated claims, or by making promises that they do not intend to keep. It's commonly used as a way to suggest that someone is being dishonest and that their words should not be taken at face value.

23. Third time's the charm

The idiom "third time's the charm" is used to express the idea that the third attempt at something will be successful, often after two previous unsuccessful attempts. The origin of this phrase is likely ancient, as things that come in sets of three have often been associated with good luck due to their similarity with the Holy Trinity of Christianity. The earliest documented use of the expression in written form can be traced back to Elizabeth Barrett Browning's work, *Letters Addressed to R.H. Horne*, published in 1839, where it is noted that "The luck of the third adventure is proverbial," implying that the expression was already in widespread usage during that era. The saying is commonly employed in a jovial and hopeful manner, implying that persistence will lead to eventual triumph.

24. Hook line and sinker

To fall for something "hook, line, and sinker" means that someone has completely and uncritically accepted someone else's deception or lies. The phrase originated from the world of fishing, where a hook, line, and sinker are the basic components of a fishing rig. The hook is used to catch the fish, the line is used to reel it in, and the sinker is used to take the bait to the bottom of the water where the fish are located. The expression is thought to have come about in the late 1700s, and it is often used to indicate that someone has been completely taken in or deceived by something or someone, usually in a situation where they have been tricked or duped.

25. To pitch in

The idiom "to pitch in" is believed to have originated in the late 19th century and it refers to the act of contributing to a task or activity, usually voluntarily. It comes from the noun "pitch" which means a throw or a toss, and the preposition "in" indicating that one is participating or getting involved. The phrase originated in the mid-1800s from the practice of pitching hay or other materials onto a pile or into a barn. The term then started to be used more broadly to refer to any kind of voluntary participation or contribution to a task or activity.

26. It's not rocket science

The expression "it's not rocket science" is used to describe a task or concept that is not difficult or complicated. Rocket science is considered to be a complex and challenging field, and the phrase "it's not rocket science" is often used to contrast this complexity with something that is easier to understand or do. Most of the early citations of "not rocket science" relate to football, and the idiom has been used in this context to describe the simplicity of the game. A sports report in the Pennsylvania newspaper *The Daily Intelligencer*, from December 1985, stated: "Coaching football is not rocket science and it's not brain surgery. It's a game, nothing more."

27. In the loop and out of the loop

"In the loop" refers to being included in a group of people who are privy to important information or decision-making. The phrase originates from military terminology, where officers would communicate orders to soldiers in a feedback loop, keeping all personnel informed. If one is "in the loop," they are included in this group and have access to the specific knowledge shared among its members. On the other hand, being "out of the loop" means being excluded from this group and not having access to the information. The expression is based on the idea of a loop that goes around in a full circle, with those included in the loop being inside it, while those excluded are outside of it.

28. Waste not, want not

The origins of the phrase "waste not, want not" are not entirely clear, with various writers, speakers, and everyday people having used it for centuries. It is believed to date back to at least 1772, and the first citation of it in the United States can be traced to 1932, when it appeared in the book *Topper Takes a Trip* by T. Smith. However, it is also suggested that the idiom may date back even further to the 1500s, with an alliterative version "Willful waste makes woeful want" also in use. Despite its vague beginning, the meaning of the phrase remains relevant today, serving as a reminder to use resources wisely and avoid unnecessary consumption.

29. Twist someone's arm

To "twist someone's arm" means to persuade or coax someone, especially when it is something they are reluctant to do. It usually refers to one person pressuring another person into getting what they want. The origins of this idiom are not clear, but it's likely that it has been in use for many centuries. The phrase "twist someone's arm" suggests the use of physical force, but it is generally used in a more metaphorical sense to describe the use of persuasive techniques or tactics.

30. Witch hunt

A "witch hunt" refers to a campaign based on unfounded or exaggerated accusations, often targeting a specific group or individual. This phrase comes from the historical practice of hunting and punishing people accused of practicing witchcraft, which occurred in Europe and later in America from the 15th to 18th centuries. During these hunts, individuals, often women on the fringes of society, were accused of causing misfortunes through magic and were imprisoned or tortured. Sometimes, they were even executed without the opportunity to defend themselves against the allegations. The expression is used in a negative or critical way today, implying that the campaign or pursuit is unfair or unjust. It was first used idiomatically in the United States in the 1940s and is still commonly used today to describe situations where people are targeted or pursued based on unfounded accusations.

Did You Know?

- The word "majestic" comes from the Latin "majestas," which means "greatness" or "dignity." It describes something that is grand, stately, or impressive.
- The word "samurai" comes from the Japanese "saburau," which means "to serve." It was used to describe a member of a class of Japanese warriors who were trained in martial arts and were known for their bravery and loyalty.
- The word "bamboo" comes from the Kannada "bambu," which is the name of a type of grass that is native to India. It is a type of woody plant with hollow stems that are used for a variety of purposes, including building materials, food, and decorative items.
- The word "shampoo" comes from the Hindi "champoo," which means "to press." It refers to a product that is used to clean the hair and scalp.

31. Not all it's cracked up to be

The expression "not all it's cracked up to be" has its origins in an archaic meaning of the verb "crack," which was used to describe excessive boasting. This usage of "to crack" was prevalent during the late 18th and early 19th centuries. The phrase suggests that if something is touted as being superior, and subsequently fails to live up to that reputation, it can be said to not be all it's cracked up to be. This idiomatic expression is exemplified in the quote from the American frontiersman and politician Davy Crockett, who stated, "Martin Van Buren is not the man he is cracked up to be."

32. A class act

To be "a class act" means that a person is of high quality or that they demonstrate good manners, taste, or style. The phrase probably originated in the mid-20th century in the context of the entertainment industry, particularly in theater and movies. The expression is often used to praise individuals who have a strong sense of style, elegance, and professionalism, and are gracious, considerate, and well-mannered, treating others with respect and courtesy. It is also used to describe a performance, an event, or a product that is of high quality and well-executed. To understand the root of this idiom, it's important to consider the evolution of the word "class." In the 17th century, the term "class" was used to define status within a divided society. This use of the word is still common today, accompanied by the terms "higher," "middle," "lower," and "working." It wasn't until 1874 that the definition gained new usage in print, when John Hotten's Dictionary defined "class" as "The highest quality or combination of highest qualities among athletes."

33. Snug as a bug in a rug

The idiom "snug as a bug in a rug" refers to a situation in which someone is comfortable, warm, and secure, often in reference to being in bed or wrapped in a blanket. It is thought to have originated in the 19th century and is likely derived from the idea of a bug or insect being warm and secure inside a rug or blanket. Now, the phrase is used more broadly to describe any situation in which someone is comfortable, whether it is at home in bed or simply feeling at ease in a social or work setting. The expression is a common idiom in English and is often used to convey a sense of relaxation or contentment.

34. A little bird told me

The phrase "a little bird told me" is used to describe information that has been obtained through insider knowledge or through hearing something from an unknown source. The idiom originated in the early 20th century and is often used as a metaphor for a confidential source of information. However, an alternative theory suggests that it may have been derived from the use of messenger birds and pigeons. Additionally, in Norse legend, Sigurd could hear and understand the birds after he slayed the dragon Fafnir, where the birds warned him that Regin would kill him.

35. A penny saved is a penny earned

"A penny saved is a penny earned" is used to express the idea that saving money is just as valuable as earning it. The phrase is believed to have originated in the 18th century and is often attributed to Benjamin Franklin, who included a similar saying in his 1737 book, *Poor Richard's Almanack*. The expression is used to encourage thrift and financial responsibility, suggesting that saving money is just as important as working for it.

36. Actions speak louder than words

The saying "actions speak louder than words" means that what a person does is more important than what they say. It suggests that a person's actions give a better understanding of their true beliefs, goals, and character compared to their words. This proverb has been around for a long time and can be found in many languages. It was first recorded in English in 1736 in a piece called "Melancholy State of Province" and says, "Actions speak louder than words, and are more to be regarded."

37. Blue once a month

The expression "blue once a month" is used to describe a person who is prone to feeling sad or depressed. It is thought to have originated in the United States in the early 20th century and has been in use in the English language for many decades. The phrase likely comes from the concept of "the blues," a term used to describe a feeling of sadness or melancholy. It is possible that the idiom "blue once a month" was originally used to describe someone who experienced these feelings on a regular, possibly monthly basis. Today, the phrase is used more broadly to describe someone who is prone to feeling sad or depressed, regardless of how often these feelings occur. It's often used in a casual or lighthearted manner, implying that the person's feelings of sadness are not particularly severe or persistent.

38. To bell the cat

"To bell the cat" means to take on a risky or dangerous task, especially one that is necessary but that others are unwilling to do. It often describes a situation where someone volunteers to do something that is difficult or risky, even though there is a possibility of failure or negative consequences. The origins of this idiom can be traced back to a fable about a group of mice who were being terrorized by a cat. The mice decided that they needed to find a way to protect themselves from the cat, and they came up with a plan to put a bell around the cat's neck so that they would always be able to hear it coming. However, when it came time to put the plan into action, none of the mice wanted to be the one to approach the cat and put the bell on it. The fable ends with the moral that it is easy to suggest solutions to problems, but it is much harder to actually take the necessary actions to solve them.

39. Dig one's heels in

The origins and history of the idiom "dig one's heels in" is rooted in the physical action of a person or animal resisting forward motion by leaning backwards and digging their heels into the ground. It is thought to have developed as a metaphor for someone who is stubborn or determined not to give in or change their stance on something. The phrase has been in use since the early 20th century and is commonly used to describe someone who is unwilling to compromise or budge on a particular issue.

40. The best thing since sliced bread

"The best thing since sliced bread" means something that is very good or innovative. It is often used to describe an invention that has made life easier or more convenient. The origin of this idiom is attributed to the invention of the bread-slicing machine in 1928. Before this time, bread was typically sold unsliced and had to be cut by hand. The bread-slicing machine made it much easier and more convenient to slice bread, and it became extremely popular.

Did You Know?

- The word "set" has the highest number of definitions in the English language, with over 430. It can be used as a noun, verb, adjective, or adverb and can mean anything from a group of objects to a direction in which something is placed.
- The word "run" is the most common verb in the English language and it can be used in a wide range of contexts, including physical movement, the operation of a machine or system, and the performance of a task.
- The word "love" is the most common noun in the English language and it can refer to a variety of emotions, including affection, kindness, and attachment.
- The word "yoga" comes from the Sanskrit "yuj," which means "to yoke" or "to unite." It is a system of physical, mental, and spiritual practices that originated in ancient India and is designed to help achieve a state of balance and inner peace.
- The word "tattoo" comes from the Tahitian "tatau," which means "to mark."
- The word "ghoti" is a humorous way of illustrating the quirks of the English spelling system. It is pronounced "fish," but it is spelled using the "gh" from "enough," the "o" from "women," and the "ti" from "nation."

41. Under the table

The expression "under the table" typically refers to something that is being done secretly or covertly. It can also mean something that is being done illegally or in violation of the rules or laws, such as in bribery or kickbacks. The phrase comes from the image of people passing money under a table so that others cannot see the exchange. This idiom has been in use since the mid-1900s.

42. Not your cup of tea

The idiom "not your cup of tea" is a metaphor that refers to the idea that everyone has different tastes and preferences, just like how people might prefer different types of tea. It is often used to politely decline an offer or suggestion, indicating that something is not to one's liking. The phrase is thought to have originated in Britain at the beginning of the 20th century, although the affirmative version (meaning something is to one's liking) was already in use at least as far back as the mid 18th century. The phrase "a cup of tea" was originally used to describe a favored friend. The expression was first used by the working class and became more widely known after appearing in William de Morgan's 1908 novel *Somehow Good*. By 1932, the expression was well-known enough to be used in Nancy Mitford's comic novel *Christmas Pudding* without any need for explanation.

43. To get on like a house on fire

"To get on like a house on fire" means to get along very well or to have a strong and harmonious relationship. It originated in the 19th century and may have originally been used to describe the idea of two people or groups forming a close relationship. In modern usage, the phrase commonly describes situations where two people or groups are able to communicate effectively and form a strong bond. It suggests that two people or groups have a strong and positive connection with one another, and are able to communicate and cooperate effectively as a result. It's thought to have been inspired by the idea of a house that is on fire, which suggests a situation that is intense or passionate.

44. Close, but no cigar

The idiom "close, but no cigar" describes a situation where someone comes close to achieving something but ultimately falls short of success. It is believed that the origin of the phrase can be traced back to the mid-20th century in the United States, when carnival exhibitions would offer cigars as rewards. Players had to win a game to receive a cigar, and those who came close but didn't win would be told "close, but no cigar" or "nice try, but no cigar." The phrase has since been used in various contexts, usually in a lighthearted and humorous way to describe someone who has come close but hasn't quite achieved success.

45. No horse in the race

The phrase "no horse in the race" (and no dog in the fight) means to have no stake or interest in a particular event or outcome. The phrase originated from horse racing, where each competitor is represented by a horse. If someone had no horse in the race, it means they have no horse competing and therefore no stake in the outcome. It's often used in a more general sense to indicate a lack of involvement or interest in a situation. This idiom has been used in print since the late 19th century.

46. Under the weather

The expression "under the weather" refers to a temporary state of feeling unwell. It has its origins in nautical terminology, where it was used to describe sailors who had become ill or seasick due to the harsh weather conditions at sea. To recover, these sailors were typically sent to the most stable part of the ship, which was located under the weather rail. The phrase conveys the idea that the individual is affected by the weather, and it was used to describe a variety of symptoms associated with seasickness, including nausea, dizziness, and a general feeling of malaise. It is important to note that the expression is not limited to describing physical illness, it can also be used to express a more general feeling of depression.

47. Good things come to those who wait

"Good things come to those who wait" is an idiom that means that positive outcomes will eventually be achieved by those who are patient and persistent. It originated in the 16th century and was inspired by the idea that good things often require time and effort to achieve, and that those who are willing to wait and put in the necessary effort will eventually be rewarded. In modern usage, the phrase is often used to encourage patience and perseverance and to keep working towards the goals, even when faced with challenges or setbacks.

48. Turn a deaf ear

To "turn a deaf ear" means to refuse to listen or pay attention. It is often used to describe a situation in which one intentionally ignores a request or suggestion, or fails to listen to what someone else is saying. The phrase was first recorded in the early 1400s by Walter Hylton, who wrote, "Make deef ere to hem as though thou herde hem not." Since then, versions of the expression have appeared in many proverb collections, from John Heywood's collection in 1546 to James Kelly's collection in 1721.

49. Fish story

"Fish story" is a term that refers to a tall tale or an exaggerated account. It originated with fishermen, who were known for telling humorous or entertaining stories about the size or number of fish that they had caught, even if those stories weren't entirely true. In modern usage, the phrase is often utilized more broadly to describe any exaggerated story, regardless of whether it's related to fishing. It's often used to gently tease or mock someone who is telling an unbelievable story as a way to suggest that the story may not be entirely factual or accurate. Overall, "fish story" is a playful way to describe a story that may be exaggerated or not entirely accurate.

50. Flesh and blood

The origin of the phrase "flesh and blood" can be traced back to the early translation of the Bible into Old English. Specifically, it appears in the Anglo-Saxon Gospels, Matthew 16:17, which was written around 1000 AD. The term in Old English is "hit ye ne onwreah flaesc ne blod," which was later translated in the King James Bible as "Flesh and blood hath not revealed it unto thee." By the time Shakespeare arrived on the scene, "flesh and blood" had already become a commonly-used phrase and its meaning was well established. The idiom emphasizes the human condition and how we are all just frail, biological beings.

Did You Know?

The Canterbury Tales is a collection of stories written in Middle English by Geoffrey Chaucer in the late 14th century. It is widely considered one of the greatest works of English literature and a cornerstone of medieval storytelling.

The Canterbury Tales consists of twenty-four tales, each told by a different narrator who is part of a group of travelers making a pilgrimage to the shrine of Thomas Becket in Canterbury, England. The stories range in genre from bawdy anecdotes and courtly love tales to moral allegories and religious narratives.

Each tale is unique in style, tone, and subject matter, offering a diverse representation of medieval society. Chaucer's depiction of his characters is vivid and engaging, showcasing their personalities, motivations, and flaws. The narrator of each tale reflects their own social status, upbringing, and education, providing insight into the cultural and literary traditions of the time.

One of the most famous tales in the collection is "The Knight's Tale," a chivalric romance that recounts the story of two knights who fall in love with the same woman. Another well-known tale is "The Wife of Bath's Tale," which tells the story of a bawdy woman who educates her fifth husband on the true nature of women.

In addition to its literary significance, *The Canterbury Tales* is also considered a landmark in the history of the English language. Chaucer's use of Middle English, a transitional stage between Old and Modern English, makes the tales accessible to modern readers while preserving the flavor of medieval language and culture.

51. To be on the same wavelength

"To be on the same wavelength" means to be in agreement or to have a shared understanding. It originated in the early 20th century and described the idea that two people or groups are able to understand one another's thoughts or intentions. The phrase is thought to have been inspired by the concept of radio waves, which are used to transmit and receive information, and the idea that two radios that are "tuned" to the same frequency will be able to communicate with one another. In modern usage, it suggests that two people or groups have a shared perspective on something, and are able to communicate effectively because of that shared understanding.

52. Every nook and cranny

The idiom "every nook and cranny" has been utilized since the early 19th century and refers to thoroughly searching every small or concealed location. The phrase is thought to have originated from the maritime term "nook," denoting a small corner or alcove, and "cranny," meaning a tiny fissure or crevice. Both of these terms have been in use since the 14th century. The earliest documented occurrence of the idiom can be found in the 1803 publication of the book *Scottish Scenery* by James Cririe, in which the following verse is written: "The piercing frost, the mass of drifted snow, that smooths the valley with the higher ridge, and ev'ry winding nook and cranny fills?"

53. Eat like a bird

The idiomatic phrase "eat like a bird" is used to describe someone who eats very little, usually referring to a small or dainty person. The expression originated in the early 20th century and likely refers to the small size and delicate eating habits of birds. However, this simile alludes to the mistaken impression that birds don't eat much (they actually do, relative to their size), and dates from the first half of the 1900s. An antonym of this phrase is "eat like a horse," which dates from the early 1700s, and alludes to the tendency of horses to eat whatever food is available. This idiom is used to describe someone who eats a lot or eats in large quantities.

54. Straw that broke the camel's back

The famous idiom "the straw that broke the camel's back" refers to a small, seemingly insignificant event or action that, when added to a series of previous events, causes a situation to become unbearable or a problem to become insurmountable. It is often used to describe a circumstance where someone has been subjected to a series of small, incremental stresses or difficulties, and the final straw is the one that causes them to snap or reach their breaking point. The origin of the phrase can be traced back to ancient times and the practice of camel caravans in the Middle East. Camels are capable of carrying heavy loads, but their backs are not designed to withstand an infinite amount of weight. If a camel's back is already loaded with a heavy pack, and then an additional straw is added, it can cause the camel's back to give out. This idiom was first recorded in print in the 18th century.

55. Bounce something off someone

The expression "bounce something off someone" means to discuss something informally, usually to get another person's opinion or feedback. It is often used as a way to test out an idea or get someone's perspective on a matter before making a decision or taking further action. The phrase suggests the idea of tossing an idea or question back and forth between people in order to get different viewpoints and insights. The metaphor underlying this idiom was described in a 1956 newspaper, which stated that ideas have a lot in common with rubber balls, in that the way they bounce depends on various factors such as the starting point, the force with which they were thrown, the character of the surface they hit, and the ambient temperature. All of these factors can influence the bounce of a ball and the rebound of an idea. This idiom is often used in a casual or informal setting, such as when brainstorming ideas or seeking advice from a colleague or friend.

56. We'll cross that bridge when we get to it

"We'll cross that bridge when we get to it" means that one will deal with a problem or issue when it arises, rather than worrying about it in advance. It is often used as a way to reassure someone or to indicate that there is no need to worry about something until it becomes necessary. Even though the origin of the phrase is not known, it has been utilized since before the 1800s when long travels were done on foot or horseback and crossing bridges was a common occurrence. The reliability of faraway bridges was not guaranteed, so crossing a bridge was considered a risky matter and a metaphor for solving problems. The adverb "when" indicates that the event is anticipated to take place in the future, while the conjunction "if" introduces a conditional clause, indicating that the event is not inevitable. The first recorded use of the idiom can be found in Henry Wadsworth Longfellow's *The Golden Legend* (1851): "Don't cross the bridge till you come to it, is a proverb old and of excellent wit." The phrase is often changed to "I'll cross that bridge if I come to it."

57. Don't rain on my parade

The idiom "rain on someone's parade" means to spoil or ruin someone's plans or enjoyment. The phrase is typically used as a verb, as in "Don't rain on my parade," which means "Don't try to spoil my plans or enjoyment of something." It can also be used as a noun, as in "She was a real rain on the parade." The expression frequently describes someone who is overly critical or pessimistic and has a tendency to bring others down. The saying is thought to have originated in the United States in the early 20th century and is said colloquially in a lighthearted or humorous way. One theory is that it refers to the tradition of parades, which are often held outdoors and are subject to the weather. If it starts to rain during a parade, it can ruin the event and dampen the mood of the participants and spectators. Another theory is that it is derived from the phrase "pour cold water on," which means to spoil or ruin something.

58. Take a rain check

The saying "take a rain check" is used to indicate that one will accept a future opportunity instead of the current one that is being offered. The phrase originated in the late 19th century from the world of baseball, where a "rain check" was a ticket that could be used to attend a game that was rained out, and thus, could not be completed. The expression is often used in the context of social invitations or events, where one can't attend the event but would like to attend the next time. It's a polite way of declining an invitation without offending the host. The idiom is also commonly used in the context of shopping or buying products, when the item is out of stock and the customer can't purchase it, they can take a rain check and buy it later.

59. Shoot oneself in the foot

To "shoot oneself in the foot" means to harm or sabotage oneself, often through one's own actions or words. It is often used to describe someone who is their own worst enemy or who unintentionally causes problems or setbacks. The phrase originates from a phenomenon that became common during the First World War, when soldiers would shoot themselves in the foot in order to be sent to the hospital tent rather than being sent into battle, claiming the shooting to be accidental. The metaphor suggests that one is causing problems or setbacks for oneself, much like these soldiers were causing harm to themselves in order to avoid battle. The earliest written use of this expression dates back to the early 20th century. It appears in *The American Language* by H.L. Mencken, which was published in 1919.

60. Hold your horses

The idiom "hold your horses" is thought to have come from the United States during the 1800s. Originally, it was written as "hold your hosses," using the American slang term "hoss" for a horse. The phrase is used to tell someone to be patient or to wait a moment before acting or speaking. It is believed to have originated from horse racing, where a jockey would tell their horse to "hold" or "stay" when waiting for the starting signal. Additionally, it could also have roots in the military as a command to stop or wait before proceeding. The expression took its current form in 1939.

Did You Know?

J.K. Rowling's *Harry Potter* series has taken the literary world by storm, enchanting readers of all ages with its magical storytelling. The first book in the series, *Harry Potter and the Sorcerer's Stone*, has been sold a hundred and twenty million copies. It introduces readers to the young wizard Harry Potter as he embarks on a journey of self-discovery and battles against the forces of darkness. This modern fantasy classic has captured the hearts of readers globally, fostering a community of fans and igniting a renewed interest in reading among young audiences.

Don Quixote by Miguel de Cervantes is a literary masterpiece that has captured the imagination of readers for centuries. This novel follows the adventures of the delusional yet endearing Don Quixote as he tilts at windmills and quests for chivalrous ideals. Renowned for its wit, satire, and exploration of the nature of reality, *Don Quixote* laid the foundation for modern fiction and remains a beloved classic that has inspired countless works of literature. This novel has sold over five hundred million copies.

The Bible stands as one of the most popular and influential books of all time, shaping the beliefs, ethics, and cultures of millions around the world. Its stories, teachings, and historical accounts have provided guidance and inspiration for generations, impacting art, literature, and even political thought. The Bible continues to be a source of spiritual and moral insight, making it an enduring cornerstone of human literature. The Bible has sold anywhere between five and seven billion copies.

These three books – *Harry Potter and the Sorcerer's Stone*, *Don Quixote*, and The Bible – have each left an indelible mark on the literary landscape, captivating readers and influencing the way stories are told and experienced.

61. Raise one's hackles

To "raise one's hackles" means to become defensive or aggressive, often as a result of feeling threatened or offended. The phrase originated in the 19th century and it comes from the physical reaction of certain animals, such as dogs, when they feel threatened or aggressive. When animals feel threatened, their body hair (or hackles) will stand up, making them appear larger and more intimidating. This physical reaction is known as "raising the hackles," and it is thought to be a sign of aggression or defensiveness. The idiom is often used to describe human behavior as well, particularly when someone becomes aggressive in response to a perceived offense or danger.

62. Don't put all your eggs in one basket

The expression "don't put all your eggs in one basket" is used as a warning against putting all of one's resources into a single venture or relying too heavily on one thing. The phrase suggests that if all of one's eggs, or resources, are placed into a single basket, and that basket is lost or destroyed, all of the eggs (resources) will be lost as well. This idiom comes from an old proverb, most likely Spanish or Italian, and was first found in print during the 17th century. The phrase appears in *Don Quixote* by Miguel de Cervantes in 1615 who wrote, "It is the part of a wise man to keep himself today for tomorrow, and not venture all his eggs in one basket." It's also found in *A Common Place of Italian Proverbs and Proverbial Phrases* by Giovanni Torriano in 1666 and is similar to an older proverb, originally in Latin: "Venture not all in one ship."

63. Between a rock and a hard place

"Between a rock and a hard place" is used to describe a situation in which someone is faced with two difficult or undesirable options and is unable to choose between them. It suggests that they are in a difficult or impossible predicament, and that either choice they make will have negative consequences. The origin of this phrase can be traced back to early 1900s America and a dispute between copper miners and mining companies in Arizona. The miners sought better working conditions and the companies refused to provide. This created a dilemma for the miners, who were faced with two unsavory options: endure the same grueling conditions (a rock), or face unemployment and poverty (a hard place). The idiom gained widespread usage during the Great Depression of the 1930s, as many individuals found themselves in a similar situation, caught between a rock and a hard place, due to the dire economic conditions of the time.

64. Sit on the fence

To "sit on the fence" refers to a neutral or impartial stance in a situation, characterized by the avoidance of taking a side or making a decision. The origin of this phrase is uncertain, but it is believed to have emerged in the late 19th century. One theory suggests that the expression is derived from the image of a person physically sitting on a fence, which serves as a barrier that separates two sides. This metaphor implies that the person is neither choosing a side nor making a decision. Another theory posits that it may have originated from the practice of people sitting on fences to observe disputes or arguments without becoming involved. This behavior, known as "spectating," is thought to have influenced the adoption of the idiom to describe a similar behavior in human interactions.

65. To cut someone some slack

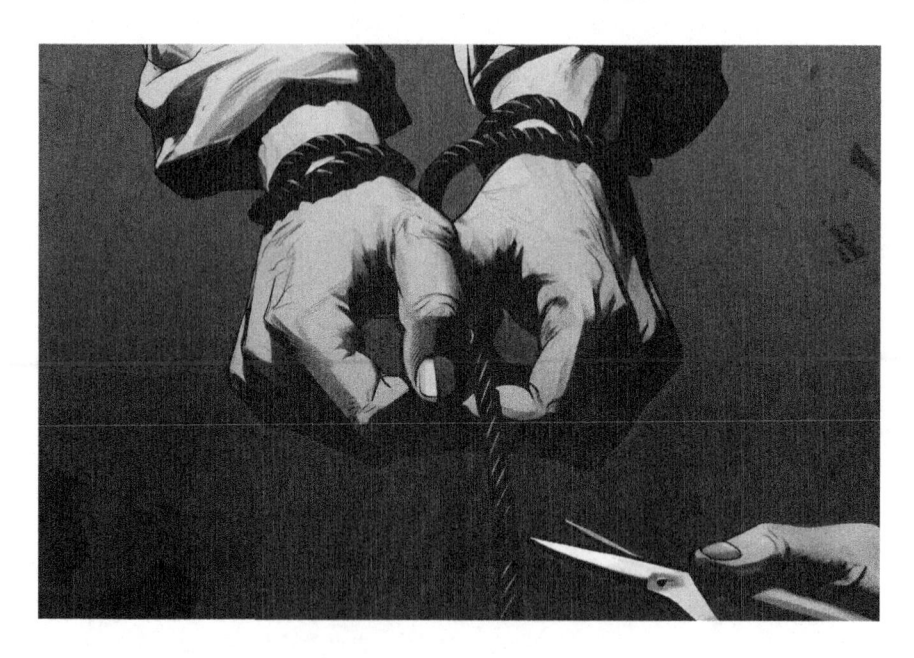

The idiom "cut someone some slack" is an informal expression that means to be understanding and forgiving towards a person, and to give them some leeway or understanding. It is often used to encourage someone to relax or not be too hard on themselves or others. This expression originated around the mid-1900s and is thought to allude to the slackening of tautness in a rope or sail. The word "slack" has a rich history, with its earliest known usage dating back to the 1300s. In this time, the word meant cessation of pain or grief. However, the idiom "cut someone some slack" does not come from this definition of the word. Instead, it comes from the word's other definition, which refers to the loose part of a sail or rope. This definition dates back to the late-1700s.

66. Spice things up

To "spice things up" means to make something more interesting, exciting, or lively. It can be used in many different contexts, such as in a relationship, a conversation, a party, or a situation that has become monotonous. The phrase is thought to have originated from the use of spices in cooking, where a spice is a substance added to food or drink to intensify the flavor. Spices are usually aromatic and robust to the taste and many spices are well known to have medicinal or alchemical properties. The word "spice" comes from Latin, "species" (plural) meaning "spices, goods, wares" and in classical Latin, it meant "kind, sort." In Old French it was written as "espice" and the modern version modified it to "épice." The expression "to spice things up" emerged as a figurative meaning, since the nature of herbs was used to improve the flavor and enjoyment of food. This meaning is believed to have originated around the 1520s.

67. To get a second wind

The expression "to get a second wind" suggests that a person is able to find an additional source of energy or strength, as if they are able to take a deep breath and keep going. It usually refers to a scenario where someone is able to overcome a challenge or obstacle by finding a renewed sense of energy or determination. This idiom has been in use since the late 1800s and originally referred to the return of a regular breathing pattern after any kind of physical effort. Long-distance runners often do get a "second wind" at some point in a race when they find it easier to breathe. In *The Franchise Affair* (1946), Josephine Tey wrote: "Perhaps it was the presence of an ally… or perhaps she had just got her second wind."

68. Elbow grease

The term "elbow grease" refers to the physical effort and hard work that is required to complete a task or achieve a goal. It is often used to describe the effort that is needed to clean or maintain something, such as scrubbing a floor or polishing a car. The phrase suggests that one must be willing to put in a lot of hard work and exert themselves in order to get a job done, and that this may involve using one's hands and arms to apply force or pressure. The idiom is thought to have originated in the early 19th century and it may have come from the idea of using one's elbow to apply force or pressure when scrubbing or cleaning. The phrase is commonly said as encouragement for someone to work hard and to persevere even when a task is difficult.

69. Smoke and mirrors

The idiom "smoke and mirrors" describes a situation where deception or manipulation is used to create an illusion or distract attention from the truth. The phrase originated from the world of stage magic and illusion, where smoke and mirrors were used to create the illusion of objects appearing or disappearing. The technique was first documented as early as 1770 and became popular after its use by the charlatan Johann Georg Schröpfer. It was a staple in 19th-century phantasmagoria shows. Phantasmagoria was a genre of horror theater that employed the use of one or multiple magic lanterns to cast haunting images, including skeletons, demons, and ghosts onto walls, smoke, or translucent screens. The illusion was achieved through the utilization of a secret projector, referred to as a magic lantern, which projected light through a mirror and into a cloud of smoke, dispersing the beam and producing the image.

70. Give them a run for their money

The phrase "give them a run for their money" describes the act of competing fiercely or giving a strong effort in a competition or challenge. It originated in the early 20th century and comes from horse racing. If a horse is withdrawn from a race, past a certain point, the punters who have bet on it lose their money, which makes the trainer, the stable, and the owner very unpopular with the betting public. In order to avoid this, the trainer may keep a horse that is not at its best in the race, giving the backers "a run for their money" even if the chances of winning are poor. The first recorded use of this expression in this context was in 1874.

Did You Know?

The Great Barrier Reef, located off the coast of Australia, is the world's largest coral reef system, stretching over 1,400 miles (2,253 kilometers). This incredible ecosystem is composed of thousands of individual reefs and islands, offering a home to an astonishing diversity of marine life, including vibrant coral formations, tropical fish, sharks, and sea turtles. The Great Barrier Reef is a UNESCO World Heritage Site and is recognized for its ecological significance and global importance. However, it is also under threat due to factors such as coral bleaching caused by rising sea temperatures.

The Tower of Pisa, known worldwide for its distinctive tilt, is a freestanding bell tower located in Pisa, Italy. The tower's construction began in the 12th century and was characterized by a foundation sinking into the soft ground, leading to its iconic lean. It stands at about 186 feet (fifty-six meters) tall and consists of several stories adorned with intricate white marble designs. Despite its unintended tilt, the Tower of Pisa has become a symbol of architectural curiosity and draws millions of visitors from around the globe.

Mount Everest, Earth's highest mountain, reaches an elevation of 29,032 feet (8,849 meters) above sea level. Situated in the Himalayas between Nepal and China, its towering peak has captivated the imaginations of climbers and adventurers for decades. Scaling Mount Everest is a challenging and dangerous feat due to extreme altitudes, unpredictable weather, and treacherous conditions. The mountain's allure, however, persists, and the region has become a focal point for mountaineering expeditions and exploration.

71. See a man about a dog

The idiom "see a man about a dog" or "see a man about a horse" is used as a polite or evasive way of saying that one needs to leave or go somewhere without providing a specific reason. The phrase is often used as a way of excusing oneself from a conversation or situation without giving any details about where one is going or what one is doing. The first recorded usage of this idiom can be traced back to the play *Flying Scud* written by Dion Boucicault in 1866, in which a character employs the phrase as a means of nonchalantly avoiding a problematic situation, stating, "Excuse me Mr. Quail, I cannot linger; I must attend to a matter concerning a canine." It is believed that the idiom "see a man about a dog" was originally utilized to refer to the act of procuring or disposing of a dog, which was considered a routine and unremarkable task. Analogously, "see a man about a horse" is thought to have alluded to the act of purchasing or disposing of a horse.

72. Get off your high horse

When telling someone to "get off their high horse," you ask them to stop acting so pompous. One of the earliest uses of the term is from 1380 in John Wyclif's English Works, "Ye emperour...made hym & his cardenals ride in reed on hye ors." The line refers to warhorses, which were immense, powerful creatures. The higher up in military ranks a person was, the bigger their horse would be to announce the status of the rider visually. Despite its mention in the late 1300s, the metaphorical phrase came into use in the mid-to-late 1700s.

73. Scratch someone's back

The phrase "to scratch someone's back" is an idiomatic expression that refers to a mutually beneficial relationship. It describes a situation where one does a favor or provides help for someone in exchange for the expectation that the person will do the same for them in the future. The origins of the phrase are rooted in the English Navy during the 1600s. During this time, a punishment for crew members involved being tied to the mast and lashed. To ease the severity of this punishment, the crew members would make a deal among themselves to deliver light lashes, effectively just "scratching the offender's back." The shortened version of this expression was first recorded in 1704.

74. Put something on the map

To "put something on the map" refers to making something known or famous, bringing attention to it, or making it a popular destination or topic. It originated in the early 1900s, and it comes from the idea of marking a location on a map to show that it is known or important. The phrase alludes to the idea that something or someone that was previously unknown or insignificant has become famous. It was first used to describe a town or city that had grown to the point that it is important enough to be included on a map. This could be in terms of population, economic activity, or other factors that make it a significant location.

75. Scrape the barrel

The expression "scrape the barrel" refers to a situation where the available options or resources are of low quality or are running out. It originated in the 19th century when barrels were used to store and transport goods, and "scraping the barrel" meant scooping out the last remnants of a substance from the bottom. Now, the phrase is often used figuratively to describe a situation where the available options or resources are limited or low quality. It's often used to convey a sense of desperation or a lack of alternatives.

76. A watched pot never boils

The idiom "a watched pot never boils" conveys the impatience we often feel when waiting for something to happen. It suggests that when we're anxiously monitoring a process, time seems to crawl by, making the anticipated event feel even more distant. The saying's origins can be traced back to the 16th century, when cooking was more laborious and required constant attention. While its first written use isn't precisely documented, the phrase's essence has endured. In modern times, it's used beyond the kitchen, serving as a reminder that incessantly waiting for something can make it feel slower to arrive. Today, we invoke this idiom to encourage a more patient outlook, reminding ourselves and others that allowing events to unfold naturally can ultimately make the wait more bearable and the outcome sweeter.

77. Between the devil and the deep blue sea

The idiom "between the devil and the deep blue sea" paints a vivid picture of being caught in a difficult, no-win situation with two equally undesirable options. This maritime-inspired expression has its origins in the nautical world, where sailors faced the treacherous choice of staying aboard a ship plagued by an oncoming storm ("the devil") or jumping into the uncertain depths of the open ocean ("the deep blue sea"). While the phrase's earliest recorded use in writing dates back to the 17th century, its metaphorical resonance remains potent. Today, it's a captivating way to describe being stuck between unfavorable alternatives, capturing the tension and anxiety of navigating life's tough decisions.

78. Bite the hand that feeds you

The idiom "bite the hand that feeds you" conveys the notion of acting ungratefully or disrespectfully towards someone who has provided support, help, or resources. Imagine a scenario where a dog, instead of appreciating the hand that offers food, responds by biting it. This powerful imagery illustrates the idea that turning against those who aid us can be both foolish and detrimental. The origins of this expression can be traced back to classical literature, with various forms appearing in works like Aesop's fables. Its earliest recorded use in its modern form dates back to the 17th century, in a play by John Heywood. Over time, its meaning has maintained its potency, serving as a timeless reminder to acknowledge and appreciate those who assist us, and cautioning against undermining our own support systems through ingratitude. Today, we still invoke this idiom to counsel against harming relationships by failing to recognize the value of assistance or favor.

79. By the book

The idiom "by the book" encapsulates the idea of strictly adhering to established rules, protocols, or guidelines. This phrase reflects a commitment to doing things in a methodical and conventional manner, prioritizing conformity over innovation. Its origins trace back to the military, where regulations were outlined in official manuals or "books." While its earliest use isn't definitively documented, it appeared in writings as early as the 19th century. Over time, its meaning has broadened beyond the military realm to encompass any situation where adherence to predetermined procedures takes precedence. Today, "by the book" is employed to describe someone who sticks closely to the rules, often invoking a balance between efficiency and creativity or highlighting the contrast between strict adherence and flexible thinking.

80. Keep your chin up

The idiom "keep your chin up" serves as a resilient reminder to maintain a positive attitude, even in the face of challenges. Think of it as lifting your head high, almost as if you're defying adversity with a determined spirit. The phrase finds its roots in the world of boxing, where a fighter is encouraged to keep their chin up to avoid being hit. Its earliest recorded appearance in writing can be traced back to the late 19th century. Over time, the meaning has expanded beyond physical posture to embrace emotional resilience. Today, we use this expression as a supportive gesture, offering encouragement to friends or colleagues facing tough times. It's a warm nudge to stay strong, reminding us that even in the midst of difficulty, maintaining a hopeful outlook can make a significant difference.

Did You Know?

Located in Mecca, Saudi Arabia, the Abraj Al Bait Clock Tower reaches a height of 1,972 feet (601 meters), securing its place as the third tallest building in the world. Part of a complex surrounding the Masjid al-Haram, Islam's holiest mosque, this tower serves as a symbol of the city's spiritual significance. Its distinct clock faces and ornate architectural elements not only provide functional features but also reflect the intricate craftsmanship of the region. The Abraj Al Bait Clock Tower stands as a remarkable fusion of modernity and tradition.

Rising in the heart of Shanghai, China, the Shanghai Tower reaches a remarkable height of 2,073 feet (632 meters), making it the second tallest building globally. This unique skyscraper features a twisting design that not only offers striking aesthetics but also enhances its structural stability in the face of high winds. Housing commercial spaces, hotels, and observation decks, the Shanghai Tower exemplifies China's rapid urban development and commitment to cutting-edge design principles.

The Burj Khalifa in Dubai, United Arab Emirates, stands as the world's tallest building, soaring to a staggering height of 2,722 feet (828 meters). This architectural marvel dominates the city's skyline with its sleek design and state-of-the-art engineering. Its multi-use structure includes residential spaces, offices, and luxurious amenities, showcasing the epitome of modern skyscraper innovation. The Burj Khalifa's towering presence is a testament to human ingenuity and the pursuit of pushing architectural boundaries.

81. Make hay while the sun shines

The idiom "make hay while the sun shines" encapsulates the wisdom of seizing opportunities when they're presented, just as farmers harvest hay during sunny weather to ensure its quality. It's like capturing the essence of acting when conditions are ideal for success. This phrase originated in agrarian (agricultural) societies, reflecting the practicality of capitalizing on good weather for efficient crop harvesting. While its exact first use in writing isn't precisely known, it emerged in the English language during the 16th century. As time has progressed, its significance has grown beyond farming to encapsulate the broader idea of not procrastinating when circumstances are favorable. In modern times, we use "make hay while the sun shines" as a motivational reminder to act promptly and decisively, ensuring that we don't miss out on promising opportunities that come our way.

82. Not a snowball's chance in hell

The idiom "not a snowball's chance in hell" captures the essence of utter impossibility, conveying the idea that something has virtually no chance of happening. It's like suggesting that a snowball could survive in the searing heat of the netherworld. This fiery expression likely has roots in the religious imagery of eternal damnation and began to appear in literature in the 19th century. Over time, the phrase has evolved from a purely theological context to a more colloquial one, describing situations where success or achievement is incredibly unlikely. Today, we use it to humorously emphasize the extreme improbability of an event, adding a dash of fiery rhetoric to our conversations about the improbable and the impossible.

83. Out of the frying pan and into the fire

The idiom "out of the frying pan and into the fire" paints a vivid image of moving from a challenging situation to an even worse one. It's like escaping the heat of a frying pan only to find oneself in the midst of flames. This expression draws from the realm of cooking and dates back to the medieval times, when fire and frying pans were integral to daily life. Its first recorded use in writing was in John Heywood's 1546 work, "Proverbes," revealing its deep historical roots. Over time, its meaning has broadened beyond the literal context to describe any unfortunate transition from one difficulty to another. Today, the idiom offers a poetic and succinct way to convey the idea that sometimes, our attempts to escape trouble can lead us into more trouble, a cautionary tale woven into our conversations about navigating life's challenges.

84. Read someone like a book

The idiom "read someone like a book" captures the idea of understanding someone's thoughts, emotions, or intentions with remarkable ease, much like flipping through the pages of a well-worn book. It's a metaphorical lens into human perception and insight. While its exact origins remain elusive, the expression's roots can be traced back to the 19th century, a time when books were integral to culture and communication. The idiom's first known use in writing appeared in the 1920s. Over time, it has evolved from a literal connection to books to encompass a broader understanding of human behavior. Today, we use this expression playfully and conversationally, often to highlight our ability to decipher nonverbal cues, motives, or emotions, and sometimes to acknowledge the depth of our relationships or our perceptive acumen in social situations.

85. The devil you know is better than the devil you don't

The idiom "the devil you know is better than the devil you don't" encapsulates the notion that sticking with a familiar, albeit undesirable, situation is often preferable to venturing into an unknown, potentially worse one. It's a pithy reminder that the risks of change can sometimes outweigh the discomfort of the familiar. Its origins can be traced to the 16th century, with variations appearing in various languages. While its first recorded use in writing isn't pinpointed, it resonates with timeless wisdom. Over time, the phrase has expanded beyond its original context, offering guidance on risk assessment and decision-making. Today, we invoke it to consider the pros and cons of new endeavors, acknowledging that while familiarity might breed discontent, navigating the unknown carries its own set of uncertainties, a piece of sagacious advice often shared when weighing the potential outcomes of challenging choices.

86. The shoe is on the other foot

The idiom "the shoe is on the other foot" playfully captures the essence of role reversal, indicating a situation where circumstances have shifted, often resulting in a complete change of perspective or fortune. It's like swapping shoes with someone, suddenly experiencing life from their vantage point. With its origins in the 19th century, its exact first use in writing isn't definitively known. However, the phrase's metaphorical appeal has remained consistent. Over time, its meaning has expanded to symbolize any situation where power dynamics or expectations have been inverted. Today, we use this idiom to highlight the amusing or thought-provoking aspects of changing fortunes or altered positions, adding a touch of wit to conversations about shifts in roles, power, or circumstances.

87. Turn over a new leaf

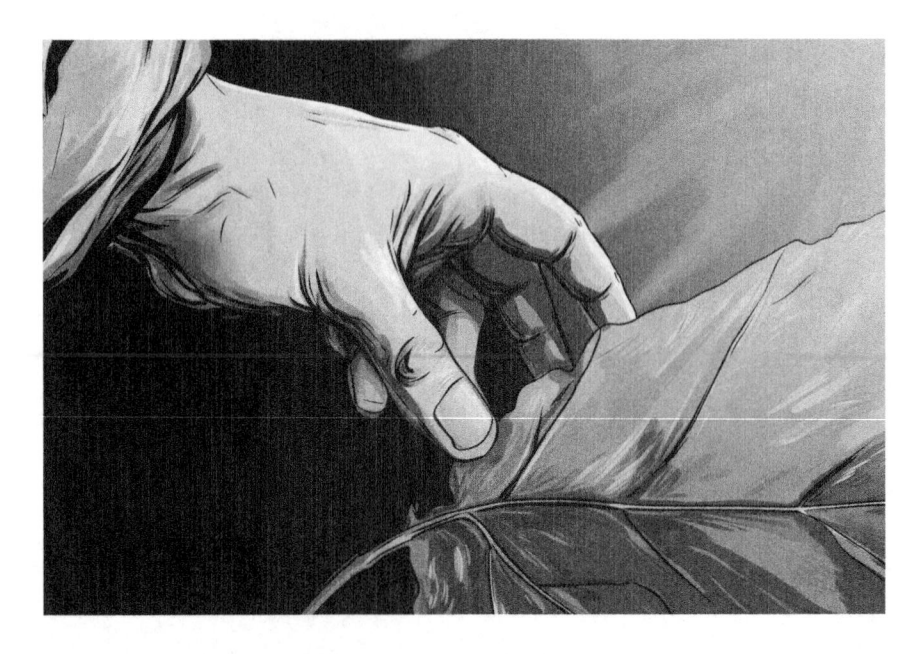

The idiom "turn over a new leaf" encapsulates the concept of making a fresh start or embracing a positive change in one's behavior or circumstances. It's like flipping to a blank page in the book of life, ready to rewrite the story. The phrase's origins can be traced back to the medieval times when books were made of leaves. While its exact first use in writing isn't precisely documented, it resonates with timeless self-improvement aspirations. Over time, the idiom has evolved from a literal reference to books to encompass personal growth and transformation. Today, this expression is used to encourage or acknowledge positive shifts in habits, attitudes, or situations, imbuing conversations with a hopeful and motivational undertone, reminding ourselves and others that change is always possible and rejuvenating.

88. Walking on air

The idiom "walking on air" captures the exhilarating sensation of extreme happiness or euphoria, akin to floating above the ground. It's like feeling so elated that your feet barely touch the earth. The phrase's origins are rooted in the idea of weightlessness, tracing back to the early 20th century. While its exact first use in writing isn't definitively known, its imagery has carried through generations. Over time, "walking on air" has expanded beyond its literal connection to flying and levity, to encompass any scenario where sheer joy or contentment prevails. Today, we use the expression to depict the elation of accomplishment, romance, or positive life events, infusing conversations with an air of happiness that's almost palpable, a lightness that reflects the wonderful feeling of being on cloud nine.

89. Wear your heart on your sleeve

The idiom "wear your heart on your sleeve" paints a vivid picture of openness and vulnerability, suggesting that someone openly displays their emotions for all to see, much like a badge of honor or a symbol pinned to their sleeve. It's as if one's inner feelings are out there for the world to witness. The phrase's origins trace back to the Middle Ages, when knights wore their ladies' favor on their sleeves as a sign of devotion. While its first recorded use in writing isn't precisely documented, it appeared in Shakespeare's "Othello" in 1604, illuminating its longstanding resonance. Over time, the meaning has evolved to denote emotional transparency and authenticity. Today, we use this expresion to both praise and caution individuals who openly express their feelings, recognizing the courage it takes to do so while also highlighting the potential risks of emotional exposure.

90. When it rains, it pours

The idiom "when it rains, it pours" aptly captures the notion that challenges or difficulties often arrive in clusters, just as heavy rainfalls can suddenly intensify. It's as if life's obstacles gather momentum and pour down all at once. The origins of this expression can be traced back to a Morton Salt advertisement in the early 20th century, wherein the phrase was coined to describe the pouring ability of their salt even in humid conditions. This clever marketing has since become a part of our lexicon. Over time, the idiom's meaning has expanded to encompass various situations where multiple problems or occurrences arise simultaneously, overwhelming an individual or situation. Today, we use it to commiserate with others facing a series of challenges or to share our own experiences of navigating a flood of difficulties, acknowledging the unpredictable nature of life's ups and downs.

Did You Know?

The origin of languages is an enigmatic tale that unfolds across the vast expanse of human history. It's a story of our innate drive to communicate, connect, and make sense of the world around us. While the exact details remain shrouded in the depths of time, linguists and researchers have pieced together clues from diverse disciplines to offer insights into the birth of human languages.

At its core, language is a powerful tool that sets us apart from other species. The journey likely began with early humans using simple gestures, vocalizations, and mimicry to convey basic needs and emotions. Over time, this rudimentary communication system evolved in response to the growing complexity of human societies. Our ancestors found innovative ways to express abstract concepts, share knowledge, and build social bonds, leading to the emergence of structured language.

The development of language was intimately intertwined with our cognitive evolution. As our brains expanded in size and complexity, our ability to process and manipulate symbols also grew. This cognitive leap enabled the formation of intricate grammatical structures and the capacity for storytelling, which became essential for passing down cultural knowledge and shaping collective identities. Through a dynamic interplay of culture, cognition, and communication, languages blossomed into the rich tapestry of diversity we see today, each one a testament to humanity's remarkable journey of expression.

91. Zero in on something

The idiom "zero in on something" refers to the act of focusing intensely and precisely on a particular target or objective. It's like narrowing down your attention until you hit the bullseye with laser-like accuracy. The phrase's origins can be traced to the world of aviation and military technology during World War II, where pilots used radar technology to "zero in" on enemy targets. Its first documented use in writing dates back to the 1940s. Over time, the idiom's meaning has expanded to include any situation where one concentrates intently on a subject or goal. Today, it is used to describe a deliberate and sharp focus, whether it's in problem-solving, decision-making, or honing in on details. It's a powerful expression that encapsulates the precision and determination required to achieve one's aims.

92. Burning the candle at both ends

The idiom "burning the candle at both ends" portrays the image of someone exhausting themselves by working excessively or indulging in various activities without respite. It's as if the candle of one's energy is being consumed from both sides, rapidly depleting its light. This phrase's origins can be traced to the 18th century poem by Edmund Clerihew Bentley, where he mentioned "A man who's burning his candle at both ends." Over time, its meaning has expanded beyond its original poetic context to encompass any situation where someone is overextending themselves, often at the cost of their well-being. Today we use this expression to caution against excessive work, stress, or overcommitment, reminding ourselves and others of the importance of finding balance and preserving one's energy for sustainable success and health.

93. Count your blessings

The idiom "count your blessings" encapsulates the sage advice of taking a moment to appreciate and acknowledge the positive aspects of one's life, even in the midst of challenges. It's like stepping back to tally up the good fortune and joys that often go unnoticed. The phrase's origins can be traced to religious texts and teachings, emphasizing gratitude for life's gifts. Its earliest documented use in writing is in the 16th century, in Thomas Tallis' hymn "All praise to Thee, my God, this night." Over time, the idiom has evolved from its religious roots to a broader cultural context, urging individuals to recognize the silver linings and small victories in life. Today, it is used as a gentle reminder to shift our perspective, fostering an attitude of thankfulness and resilience in the face of adversity.

94. Every dog has its day

The idiom "every dog has its day" refers to the belief that everyone, regardless of their current circumstances, will experience a period of success, recognition, or triumph at some point in their life. It's like a reminder that even the most overlooked or underestimated individuals will eventually shine. The phrase's origins can be traced back to ancient Roman and Greek literature, where similar sentiments were expressed. Its first use in English literature dates back to the 16th century, appearing in John Heywood's collection of proverbs. Over time, the idiom has evolved from a proverbial expression to a broader motivational message, encouraging perseverance and offering hope during challenging times. Today, we use it to uplift others and ourselves, emphasizing that setbacks are temporary, and every person is capable of achieving their moment of success or recognition, regardless of their initial circumstances.

95. Fish or cut bait

The idiom "fish or cut bait" delivers a straightforward ultimatum: make a decision and take action, or step aside and let others proceed. The phrase's origins are deeply rooted in the world of fishing, where one either engages in the act of fishing or abandons the endeavor. Its earliest recorded use in writing dates back to the 19th century, reflecting its direct and practical essence. Over time, the meaning has expanded to signify the need for commitment and determination in any endeavor, highlighting the importance of taking responsibility for one's choices. Today, we use this idiom to motivate or challenge others to take decisive action, often in situations where indecision or hesitation is hindering progress. It's an expression that beckons individuals to take control of their destiny and contribute actively to their own success.

96. Hit the ground running

The idiom "hit the ground running" encapsulates the notion of starting a new endeavor with immediate and energetic action, as if you're already in full stride the moment you begin. It's like launching into a project with enthusiasm and momentum from the very start. The origins of this phrase are often attributed to the military, describing paratroopers who would jump from planes and immediately engage in combat upon landing. While its exact first use in writing isn't known, it gained prominence in the business world during the mid-20th century. Over time, its meaning has expanded beyond its military and business contexts to encompass any situation where one begins with vigor and readiness. Today, this expression to encourage a dynamic and proactive approach to new challenges, whether in work, sports, or life in general, underscoring the value of a strong and impactful beginning.

97. Keep something at bay

The idiom "keep something at bay" conjures the image of holding a threat or challenge at a distance, preventing it from getting too close or causing harm. The origins of this phrase can be traced back to hunting, where dogs would be kept at bay, or restrained, to prevent them from attacking prey until commanded. While its earliest written use is unclear, it emerged in common language during the 16th century. Over time, the meaning has broadened beyond its literal hunting context to encompass any situation where one is managing or controlling a potential problem or difficulty. Today, we use this phrase to efforts to ward off challenges or threats, underscoring the proactive strategies we employ to maintain control and ensure our safety and well-being.

98. Like shooting fish in a barrel

The idiom "like shooting fish in a barrel" refers to the idea of an exceptionally easy task or endeavor, as if you're aiming at fish trapped in a confined space, making success virtually guaranteed. The origins of this expression are rooted in the literal sense of the phrase—shooting fish in a barrel is indeed quite effortless. Its earliest recorded use in writing can be traced back to the 19th century, often associated with humorous anecdotes or hyperbolic descriptions. Over time, the idiom has expanded beyond its literal context to depict any situation that presents minimal challenge due to the overwhelming advantage or simplicity involved. Today, we use it both playfully and pragmatically to highlight tasks that require little effort, often eliciting a knowing smile from those who understand the inherent ease of the task at hand.

99. Make a long story short

The idiom "make a long story short" succinctly conveys the act of summarizing or condensing a lengthy narrative into its essential points, skipping unnecessary details to get to the core of the matter. It's like trimming down a sprawling tale into a concise and impactful version. While its precise origins are unclear, this phrase has been in use since at least the 16th century, reflecting the human inclination to simplify stories for efficiency. Over time, its meaning has remained consistent, evolving to accommodate our fast-paced communication styles. Today, we use this expression to swiftly transition from a detailed explanation to a brief conclusion, emphasizing brevity and ensuring our audience grasps the main idea without getting lost in the intricacies of a protracted narrative. It's a linguistic shortcut that keeps conversations engaging and to the point.

100. Off the beaten path

The idiom "off the beaten path" paints a picturesque scene of venturing away from the commonly traveled route, exploring uncharted territory or unconventional experiences. It's like straying from the well-trodden trail to discover hidden gems or unique adventures. Its origins are metaphorical, drawing parallels to the literal practice of choosing lesser-known trails while hiking. Though pinpointing its first use in writing is challenging, the idiom gained prominence in the 20th century, signifying a departure from the ordinary. Over time, its meaning has extended beyond physical journeys to encompass any situation where one seeks novel or unconventional avenues, often driven by a desire for authenticity or discovery. Today, we use this phrase to suggest embracing the unfamiliar, celebrating the spirit of adventure and the thrill of encountering the unexpected. It's an invitation to step beyond the routine and embrace the allure of the unknown.

Did You Know?

Shanghai, located in China, ranks as the third most populous city in the world, with a metropolitan population exceeding twenty-seven million people. This global financial center is renowned for its rapid development, cutting-edge architecture, and international influence. The city's historic waterfront, futuristic skyline, and economic significance make it a symbol of China's transformation on the world stage.

Delhi, India's capital territory, holds the distinction of being the second most populous city globally, with a metropolitan population surpassing thirty-one million people. With a rich historical heritage that spans centuries, Delhi is a city of contrasts, offering ancient monuments alongside modern skyscrapers. Its vibrant markets, religious sites, and cultural diversity contribute to its status as a thriving urban hub.

Tokyo, the capital city of Japan, stands as the most populous city in the world, with a population exceeding thirty-seven million people in its metropolitan area. This bustling metropolis is a center of culture, technology, and commerce, boasting a vibrant blend of tradition and innovation. Its efficient public transportation, diverse neighborhoods, and iconic landmarks reflect the dynamic nature of urban life on a massive scale.

These three densely populated cities – Shanghai, Delhi, and Tokyo – showcase the complexities of urban living on an unprecedented scale. Each city presents a unique blend of tradition and progress, illustrating the diverse ways in which societies adapt to accommodate the challenges and opportunities of modern urbanization.

101. One man's trash is another man's treasure

The idiom "one man's trash is another man's treasure" refers to the concept that what might be deemed worthless by one person could hold immense value for another. It's like highlighting the subjectivity of worth and the diverse ways in which individuals perceive and appreciate items or experiences. Its origins trace back to the 17th century, when John Ray penned "One man's meat is another man's poison," which inspired the modern adaptation. Over time, the idiom's scope has broadened beyond material possessions to symbolize the uniqueness of individual preferences and perspectives. Today, we use this expression to celebrate diversity, encourage open-mindedness, and remind us that there's beauty and value in the unexpected or overlooked. It's an acknowledgment of the varied ways we assign meaning to the world around us, fostering a sense of appreciation for differing viewpoints.

Bonus!

Thanks for supporting me and purchasing this book! I'd like to send you some freebies. They include:

- The digital version of *500 World War I & II Facts*

- The digital version of *101 Idioms and Phrases*

- The audiobook for my best seller *1144 Random Facts*

Scan the QR code below, enter your email and I'll send you all the files. Happy reading!

Find more of me on Amazon!

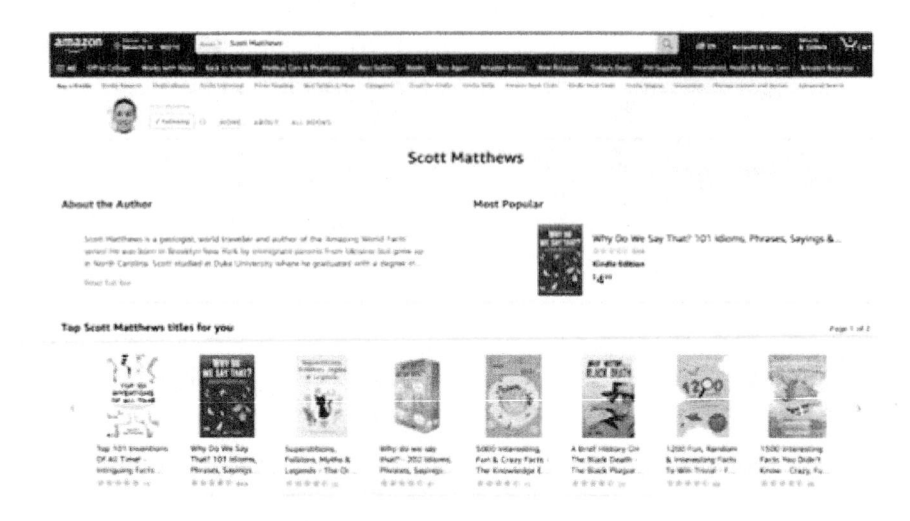

Check out the "Amazing Facts" series and learn more about the world around us!

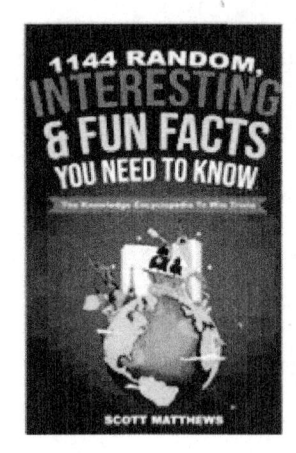

**Check out the "Why Do We Say That" series and
learn where everyday idioms and phrases come from!**

Printed in Great Britain
by Amazon